THE
Archive Photographs
SERIES

ISLINGTON

Hugh Myddleton Statue, Islington Green, N.

Islington Green in 1909 with a fine array of shops along Upper Street on its north side. The statue of Sir Hugh Myddleton surveys the High Street from its vantage point at the head of the Green. Sir Hugh brought into being the New River which carried fresh water along a conduit from Ware in Hertfordshire to the New River Head next to Sadlers Wells – there to be distributed by gravity in London. For this he earned a knighthood in 1622. Also note the tram stops close to the corners and the horse trough.

THE
Archive Photographs
SERIES

ISLINGTON

Compiled by
Gavin Smith

CHALFORD

The Chalford Publishing Company
St Mary's Mill, Chalford,
Stroud, Gloucestershire, GL6 8NX

ISBN 0 7524 0140 8

Typesetting and origination by
The Chalford Publishing Company
Printed in Great Britain by
Redwood Books, Trowbridge

Islington's famous Chapel Market which grew up to provide household provisions and necessities for the local inhabitants when the village began to spread across the fields. Seen on a typical Edwardian shopping day.

Contents

Plan of the Village of Islington in the reign of Queen Elizabeth I.

Introduction

That Islington is the hill of Gisla (a Saxon leader) can still be appreciated today. If you approach the Angel intersection from City Road or St. John Street or Goswell Road the ridge like nature of the High Street and its environs is apparent. The slope can again be seen from the Caledonian Road at the Kings Cross end, where the Regents Canal approaches its tunnel through the same hill. Before the Saxons there may have been Roman and even Celtic/British fortifications on the Barnsbury Ridge. The view over London and the Thames from Pentonville and Barnsbury, before the building of houses crowded what once were fields, was magnificent. This perspective would have given early settlers confidence in anticipating the approach of raiders from elsewhere.

Before the Romans arrived, Islington was at the base of a vast forest which stretched far away to the north (it was later known as the Forest of Middlesex). Ken Wood at Highgate is a remnant of this. The Romans began to clear a way through this for their strategic roads and camps.

The rich soil of Islington made it a natural provider of food for London as it grew, but the village was clearly a separate entity well into the nineteenth century. The original Islington village lay away from the ridge around the slopes of Essex Road near Islington Green where an irregular pattern of former narrow ways, typical of ancient settlements, can still be discerned.

Before the Norman Conquest, the foundation of St. Paul's was endowed with extensive possessions in land and property at Islington, as mentioned in its Charter. The Domesday Survey of 1086 after the Conquest mentions these lands and also others held by followers of William. The survey mentions that at Tolentone (now Highbury) there was pannage for sixty hogs and so the area must have abounded in beech and oak on which the pigs fed. A favourite chronicler of historians, the monk Fitzstephen, gives this word-picture of the country north of the London wall, in 1180: 'On the north side are fields for pasture and open meadows, very pleasant, into which the river waters do flow, and mills are turned about with a delightful noise. The arable fields are no hungry pieces of gravel ground, but like the rich fields of Asia, which plentifully bring forth corn and fill the barn of the owner with a dainty crop. ... Beyond them an immense forest extends itself, beautified with woods and groves, and full of the lairs and coverts of wild beasts and game, stags, bucks, bears and wild bulls.'

The fields which extended from the City walls all the way to Islington village were used by Londoners from an early date as places of recreation. Fitzstephen writes with enthusiasm of the athletic activities and equestrian exercises which the young people of the city enjoyed there. These sports included wrestling and archery, known as shooting the standard, broad arrow and flight. In the days when archers were important in fighting England's wars the games were part of military training.

It was not unusual in Henry VIII's time to find the King visiting the village, especially to hunt. A proclamation of 1546 stated that no person should interrupt the King's game of hare, partridge, pheasant and heron, in the country from his palace at Westminster to St Giles in the Fields, and from thence to Islington, Highgate, Hornsey, and Hampstead. An old house at Newington Green still standing in the nineteenth century was believed to have been used by the King and his party as a hunting lodge.

Queen Elizabeth I also paid visits to Islington to visit some of the gentry making their home there – a great commotion was caused on one occasion when her coach was surrounded by 'rogues'.

In the next century the fields around Islington and as far as Highgate were filled with poor homeless citizens, victims of the Great Fire of London, who camped under miserable tents and hovels having lost everything, homes and possessions, in this great tragedy of 1666. The diarist Evelyn wrote a pathetic description of this scene.

As will be seen later in this book Islington's fields became a great attraction to holidaying Londoners in the eighteenth and nineteenth centuries when many tea-gardens opened up to provide refreshment and entertainment to citizens at play.

However, once the nineteenth century got under way, the scenes of rurality depicted on such as the 1735 map soon began to give way to the late Georgian and early Victorian townscape of which remnants survive to this day.

One

The Greatest Parish
in England

Liverpool Road in 1906 with street activities against a backdrop of the impressive Agricultural Hall buildings which at the time hosted most of London's important exhibitions and events.

Dame Alice Owen's Boys' School in 1841. It was founded in 1613 with neighbouring almshouses as a thank you to Providence for a miraculous escape from death enjoyed by their foundress in her youth. The schools were rebuilt several times and the later Victorian building was extended.

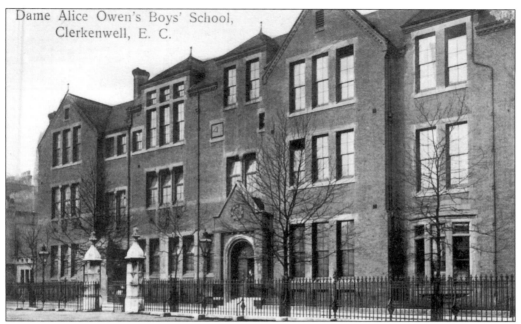

Dame Alice Owen's Boys' School,
Clerkenwell, E. C.

The school in Owen Street in 1904 – this frontage survived until comparatively recent times when the school moved away to Hertfordshire. Many generations of Owenians remember this site with affection. As you entered the building by the main door at the centre you were greeted by the Frampton statue of Lady Owen in her Tudor ruff and gown standing in an entrance hall floored in a chessboard pattern of black and white marble.

St. Mary's Infants' School, Class 2, around 1910.

The Clothworkers' Almshouses, Essex Road. This damaged print gives a good idea of this building – a rather cramped version of the Peabody Buildings style of housing. The Essex Road area was the most densely populated in Islington at the turn of the century and in some parts after the Second World War.

The Great Northern Hospital, upper Holloway Road, about 1908. Built by the Islington Vestry from a fund set up to commemorate Queen Victoria's fifty years on the throne and opened in 1888, it succeeded a smaller institution in the Caledonian Road and provided general hospital facilities for a wide and densely-populated area.

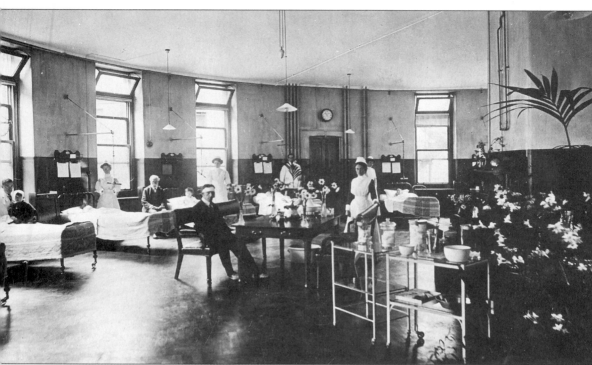

The Richard Cloudesley Ward of the hospital, 1908. Patients and nurses enjoy the diversion as the photographer operates his shutter. This ward was quite modern for its time with carefully designed windows and a decoration of cheerful plants. The hospital was renamed the Royal Northern in 1924.

St. John's Church, Finsbury Park, around 1905. Set in a pleasant residential area with wide boulevard style thoroughfares, then very quiet and traffic-free, just over the borders of the neighbouring borough, Stoke Newington.

Finsbury Park Road, leading of Seven Sisters Road, in 1906. The gates of Finsbury Park are opposite the top end, in the distance. This road is very convenient for shops, cinema, variety theatre, underground and main-line stations and walks in the park – it must have been an estate agent's dream.

5.30   44802
6.30.

6.30   2319579
7.35

915   884208.
10.10

The busy part of Highbury Park with horse buses and shops, 1904. Highbury Barn Tavern Pleasure Gardens once stood here amid the fields and woods.

Prosperous Holloway Road with the Northern Polytechnic in the middle of the view, 1905. The horse is still the main motive power for road vehicles.

High Street, Islington, 1912. This drawing by Emanuel shows the long western curve and the high pavement, considerably raised above the road.

Islington Green.

Canonbury Place, Islington, 1909, a sophisticated Edwardian street scene. It is given distinction by its mix of Georgian and later architecture – the Tower visible in the distance and the Canonbury Tavern to the right.

St. Augustine's church and Highbury New Park, 1905.

Upper Street from Highbury Corner, 1907. The Cock Tavern is on the right and the Union Chapel Tower can be seen on the left.

Kelvin Road, Highbury, a byway not often pictured, about 1910. Note the horse and cart carrying out a delivery.

The Salvation Army Citadel and Barracks, proclaiming its message to the world, Holloway, 1905.

New Court Congregational Chapel migrated to Tollington Park in 1870 from Carey Street in London at the invitation of local residents. The seating capacity was over 1300, and its frontage displayed a giant Corinthian portico. In 1960 it became St. Mellitus Catholic Church. Its splendid interior is here seen in 1906.

Islington Fire Station.

PARISH OF SAINT MARY,
ISLINGTON.

PUBLIC BATHS
AND
WASH-HOUSES.

By-Laws of the Commissioners

Made under and pursuant to

THE PUBLIC BATHS & WASH-HOUSES ACTS

AND DULY CONFIRMED BY

THE LOCAL GOVERNMENT BOARD

ON THE 25TH OCTOBER, 1892, AND 10TH FEBRUARY, 1894.

Public Baths and Wash-Houses Bye-Laws 1892/4. Issued by the Parish Vestry at a time when many houses were without their own adequate facilities for self-cleanliness and laundering. Hornsey Road Baths are seen here shortly after the Second World War. They were opened in July 1892. The Caledonian Road Baths were opened in May of the same year and the Essex Road Swimming Baths in November 1893.

Champion swimmers at Islington Baths in the Edwardian era.

Eifion Evans, the prospective Liberal candidate for West Islington at his Committee Rooms during the Parliamentary Election of 1929. Harold Bailey, the very experienced Liberal agent, is standing at the right.

West Islington Parliamentary Election,
1929

POLLING DAY, THURSDAY, MAY 30th
8 a.m. — 9 p.m.

D. EIFION EVANS
LIBERAL CANDIDATE

Election Address

Evans' election address with photograph of the candidate. The seat was won by Labour in the person of F. Montague.

Two
Canonbury and its Tower

Canonbury Tower, a link with Islington's storied past, about 1905. This romantic relic dates from the 1560s. The site once contained the Prior of St. Bartholomew in London's residence, Canonbury House, a large building constructed between 1509 and 1532. Some of the remains are still incorporated in the adjoining buildings.

Canonbury House in 1600.

Oliver Goldsmith was one of the writers who lived in the Tower from 1762–4. He frequently mentions Islington in his writings and *The Deserted Village* is thought to be a description of the place.

The Compton Oak Room in the tower. Elizabeth Spencer fell in love with William Lord Compton and is said to have eloped after being let down from the tower in a laundry basket to avoid her father's disapproval.

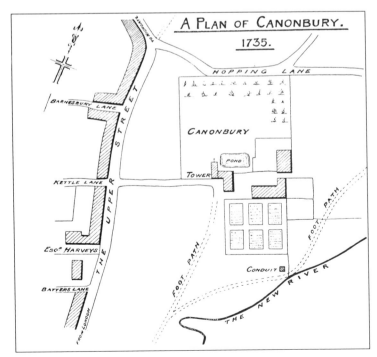

A PLAN OF CANONBURY.

1735.

A plan of Canonbury House in 1735.

The main entrance to the tower after the Second World War.

At the top of the staircase in 1908.

28

The Garden House, Alwyne Villas, 1908. This octagonal building carries on its front a 'rebus' stone, a punning heraldic reference to Prior William Bolton, who died in 1532 (the carving shows a bolt in a tun).

Canonbury House doorway, the entrance to the School House, 1908.

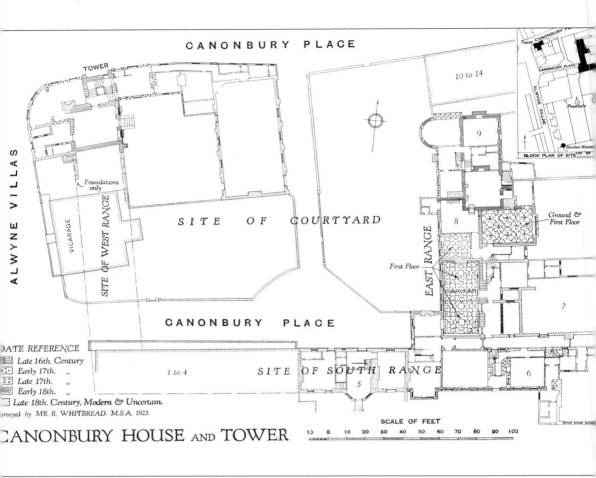

CANONBURY HOUSE AND TOWER

Canonbury House area plan, showing the extent of the old buildings.

Willow Bridge Road, Canonbury – the house at No. 13.

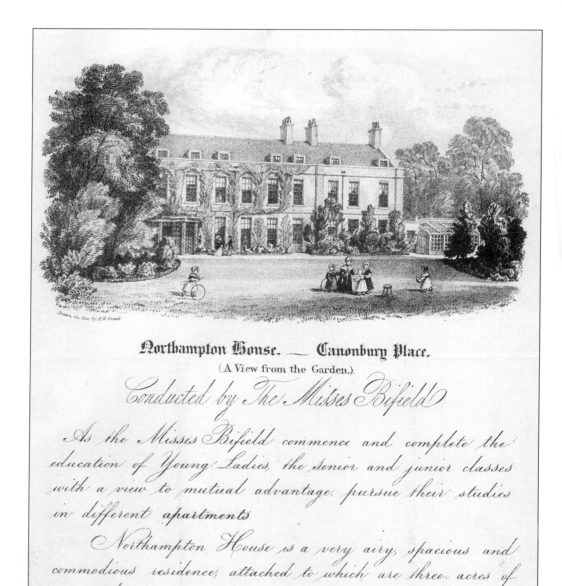

Northampton House. — Canonbury Place.
(A View from the Garden.)

Conducted by The Misses Bifield

As the Misses Bifield commence and complete the education of Young Ladies, the senior and junior classes with a view to mutual advantage, pursue their studies in different apartments

Northampton House is a very airy, spacious and commodious residence, attached to which are three acres of ground.

Northampton House School in the nineteenth century.

King Edward's Hall next to the tower, 1913. Contemporary utility vies with antique beauty of form. This hall later proved an ideal location for the Tower Theatre.

A leafy retreat: 28 Alwyne Road, 1906.

The large houses of Douglas Road face the New River in 1906.

An early petrol bus coasts along St. Paul's Road. This ancient route was originally Hopping Lane, a rural highway that lacked any footpath along its length so that weary travellers ran the risk of being run down by coaches and other vehicles.

Three
Merry Islington

The old church of St. Mary's, Islington, a church of surprising antiquity which had to be demolished with gunpowder, so strong were its foundations. At the time of this illustration, Upper Street still contained many ancient buildings such as the Pied Bull Inn and was quite picturesque with fields and haystacks in between the houses and public buildings, harking back to Tudor times and beyond.

Islington archers practicing at the Butts. The citizens of London exercised their right to improve their aim and all the fields from the City Walls to Islington were used for this purpose.

Sir Walter Raleigh's mansion at Islington.

The Queen's Head Inn, 1820.

Islington Turnpike Gate in the
nineteenth century, at the corner of
Liverpool Road and High Street.

The rebuilt church of St. Mary, Islington, a handsome Georgian building designed by Lancelot Dowbiggin and consecrated in 1754. Its tower can still be seen from the north along Upper Street, rising elegantly above the rooftops, as it has done for 240 years.

Anglers by the New River and Sadlers Wells Theatre from the engraving on Charles Dibdin's Benefit ticket.

AQUATIC THEATRE, SADLERS WELLS.

BOXA²ˢ

Nᵒ. 54

Mᴿ. C. DIBDIN'S NIGHT.

Monday, September 22ⁿᵈ 1817.

DIBDIN'S BENEFIT TICKET, SEPTEMBER 1817
Showing a view of Sadler's Wells.   196

An early Victorian view of Sadlers Wells. The proprietor of Sadlers Music House in 1683 discovered a well in the grounds which became a resort of its own and then a theatre.

Joseph Grimaldi (1779–1837), a very inventive clown, a thought up many of the traditional clown and pantomine routines. He lived near to and performed at Sadlers Wells nearly all his life and was often seen running between the Wells and other theatres where he was performing on the same evening.

Buildings at the entrance to the Highbury Barn Tavern Gardens. This place of entertainment began as a rural teahouse with the dairyman-owner selling farm fresh products to pleasure-seekers from around 1740. It ended up a mammoth pleasure resort with entertainments such as Blondin and Leotard (tightrope walkers), and a gigantic dancing platform claimed to be lit by 50,000 lamps in 1860. Highbury Barn is still the name of a bus stop although the Gardens are gone.

Islington High Street in 1840. In spite of its horse-drawn traffic, it could be quieter than the neighbourhood of Highbury Barn when the pleasure gardens were in full swing with their loud music.

The Highbury Sluice House Tavern and its footbridge over the New River. No great distance away from Highbury Barn, it was a rival attraction in the first half of the nineteenth century.

The White Conduit House, one of the many pleasure gardens in the Pentonville Road area. It was here that Mr Lord organised his first cricket club, attended by the nobility, before moving to Marylebone in 1787 to found the MCC.

Balloon.

Mr. GRAHAM

Has the honor to announce to the Public, that in consequence of the *Splendid Ascent* which gave such great Satisfaction on FRIDAY last, he has been most earnestly solicited by Mr. TURNERELLI, the celebrated Sculptor, and several Gentlemen of Science and Fashion, to make another Ascent within the Metropolis, previous to his Departure for BATH, and he has therefore fixed for

FRIDAY  NEXT,

Sept. 12th

AT THE

GARDENS

OF THE

White Conduit House,

PENTONVILLE,

When every Precaution will be taken to prevent Disappointment.

The Admission will be, as before, 3s. 6d. each; and in order to prevent any Idea of Fraud, each Person, upon payment of their Money, will receive a Check, upon Production of which, should any Failure take place, their Money will be immediately returned.

N. B. Mr. GRAHAM throws himself upon the patronage of a generous Public, and pledges himself no Expence or Exertion on his part shall be wanting to render the arrangements to give general satisfaction.   September 10, 1823.

F. P. Fargues, Printer, 47, Berwick-street, Soho.

Mr Graham's balloon ascent at the White Conduit, 12 September 1823. The conduit was set up in 1641 for the Charterhouse in the City. An ale and cakehouse was opened nearby. In 1754 Robert Bartholemew advertised his reconstructed premises with a long walk, long room, arbours, ornamental fishpond and a high fence all round to ensure privacy. More tea rooms were added in the 1770s. Fireworks were often presented as a spectacle in the first four decades of the nineteenth century. The old White Conduit was demolished in January 1849 and continued as a public house in the now built-up streets that had once been fields of delight.

The Angel Inn, Islington, in the heyday of coaching.

A panoramic view of Merry Islington taken from the outside gallery of St. Mary's Church in 1791 by John Swertner. Across the foreground runs Church Street, now called Gaskin Street

after the Revd George Gaskin. Notice the cattle, the gardens, and the fields on either side, with London in the distance.

The fields to the south of Pentonville Hill, with the nearby old mill house and Dobneys Tea Gardens. Originally Daubigny's Bowling Green, it was open as early as Spring 1718 'for the accommodation of all gentleman bowlers'. After 1760 Johnson from the Three Hats beyond the Angel pub converted it into an arena for trick horse-riding displays which he had popularised at the 'Hats'. Many variations of name were officially imposed on the pleasure resort including its original, 'The Prospect', from 1669 after its good view over London. The public however took it to their hearts as 'Dobneys'. By 1790, half the abandoned grounds were taken over for Georgian houses.

Four

Six Hundred Streets
Beneath the Sky

An Islington Carnival float passing through the Caledonian Market area in 1907. This had once been the site of Copenhagen House, a large residence said to have sheltered some Danish notable during the 1665 Great Plague. By 1700 it had become a public resort and during the reigns of the four King Georges it hosted Tea Gardens, skittles, the game of Dutch Pin and Fives – the latter was claimed to have been invented here. Copenhagen Fields were the scene for many radical gatherings, such as those in support of the French Revolution and the Tolpuddle Martyrs. By 1855 it was the site of a large cattle market and the houses and streets were moving in to surround the shrinking open spaces.

Decorated carts in the 1907 Carnival passing the railings and weirdly shaped pillar of the Caledonian Market.

Our Lady Procession, Holloway, in progress as Children of Mary bear the statue around 1911.

The wide roadway of Petherton Road (the New River originally flowed in the open down the middle and there were carriageways on either side of the railings surrounding the grassy banks – it was later covered over). This made an attractive approach for Prince Edward, later Edward VII, to visit the White House in what is now Clissard Park, over the border in Stoke Newington.

Romantic Canonbury Square with its tower, 1909.

Highbury Place, about 1905. Leading from Highbury Corner, this was developed between 1774–9 and has been the home of many famous names such as Walter Sickert, John Wesley, and Joseph Chamberlain.

Highbury Crescent, 1906. The Crescent was designed by James Wagstaffe, an Islington architect and builder. In 1846 there were only fourteen houses. It looks across Highbury Fields, an open space bought for the public in 1885, towards Highbury Place. There was once a footpath from Highbury Corner across the 'Mother Field' as it was called on the 1735 map, to the former Manor House – the upper section remains as 'Church Path'.

Highbury Terrace, 1935. Begun in 1789, Nos. 1–16 were built by 1794. Captain Joseph Huddart, an inhabitant from 1792–1816, at No. 12, was one of the elder brethren of Trinity House and laid the first stone of the East India Docks. Sir Francis Ronalds (1788–1873), one of the pioneers of the electric telegraph, lived at No. 1 – his experimental wires ran from a coach house to a nearby cottage.

No. 1024. *Mildmay Park.*

Mildmay Park in 1905. It was built in 1853–4 over the former park and pasture ground reaching almost to Balls Pond, which was acquired through marriage by Henry Mildmay, a member of Cromwell's State Council.

A house in Kelross Road, Highbury, 1911. The old name plate of Ardilaun Road, by which it was known from its completion in 1892 until 1894, remains on the wall of the house in the photograph.

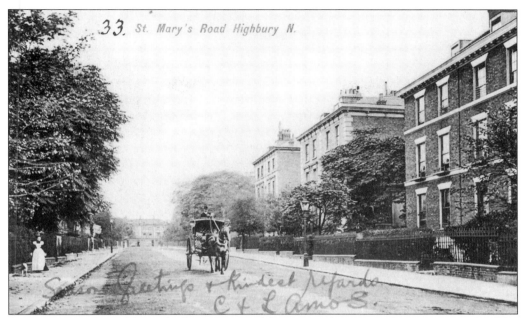

33. St. Mary's Road Highbury N.

St. Mary's Road, Highbury, built in 1848 and known as St. Mary's Grove since 1938. The Liberal Prime Minister, Henry Asquith (1908–16), had rooms here in his early days.

St. John's Villas, Upper Holloway, 1904. One can imagine the famous character from *Diary of a Nobody* living in a house like this in Holloway.

The distinctive flavour of Southgate Road in 1905 with its mixture of stuccoed houses and business premises can still be glimpsed.

Christ Church, Highbury, and the Clock Tower in 1906, which has been familiar to generations of Arsenal supporters making their way to the ground from Highbury Station, after the club's move to North London in 1913.

Witherington Road in 1908. A Victorian development of 1889.

St. James' Church, Holloway, and the neighbouring street scene in 1906.

Workaday Upper Tollington Park in 1904.

Tufnell Park Road and the distinctive façade of St. George's Church, 1904. The church, modelled after that of the Knights of St. John at Acre, became disused and was turned into a theatre in the round presenting Shakespearean and other drama of the sixteenth and seventeenth centuries from 1970.

37 Moray Road in 1905. This road was developed in 1867.

Gibson Square, 1904, one of a number of squares in the area built to an interesting design in the early nineteenth century. Developed in 1831, the ground landlords were the trustees of Thomas Milner Gibson, MP (1806–1884), a friend of Disraeli and Dickens the novelist.

Five

London's Entertainment Centre

The Liverpool Road entrances to the Agricultural hall, 1905. The 'Aggie' became a key exhibition centre for London until the advent of Earls Court and Olympia. It was the idea of the Smithfield Club to provided a splendid venue for the Cattle Shows. The building occupied almost two acres, and the foundation stone was laid during November 1861. The hall staged many trade exhibitions, motor cycle and cycle shows, early motor shows, Crufts Dog Show, the Royal Military Tournament until 1906, Revivalist meetings, concerts, balls, walking matches, circuses, and the World's Fair (a regular assemblage of a myriad forms of entertainment including a menagerie). Some of these continued into the 1930s but in 1939 the outbreak of war shut it down.

Cars galore at the 'Aggie' – the Motor Show of 1899.

Cover of the 1921 programme of the World's Fair.

the Military Tournament.

aster Tommy—"And how many men have been killed to-day, do you think, Aunty Su'? Wha good men to die for charity's sake"

At the Military Tournament – a drawing from *Fun* magazine of 25 May 1892.

A group of Coldstream Guards in the 'Dress of the Newbury Period' Tableaux await their turn at the rear of the auditorium during the Warriors of Britain Pageant, 1899, at the Royal Agricultural Hall.

Sam Collins, a 'Stage Irishman' and vocalist took over the Lansdowne Arms, Islington Green, in the 1860s. The 'Greats' all appeared here, including Charlie Chaplin. A fire in 1958 closed it.

A programme from the great days of the Collins in 1900. When films became all the rage, Collins managed to survive and Gracie Fields made her first London appearance here in a review.

The Finsbury Park Empire on its opening day, 15 September 1910.

Designed by Frank Matcham and full of red plush, the Empire was always an exciting venue for new talent, claiming to be the first house outside the London music halls.

ROYAL

PHILHARMONIC

THEATRE,

HIGH STREET, ISLINGTON.

Licensed by the Lord Chamberlain to Mr CHARLES HEAD, Proprietor,
Southside House, Tufnell Park

Under the Entire Direction of ... Mr. SHEPHERD

OPEN FOR THE SEASON,
BEAUTIFULLY REDECORATED AND EMBELLISHED.

THIS EVENING,
AND UNTIL FURTHER NOTICE,

The Performance will commence at 7.30 with a Comedietta,
entitled

The Spectre Lover!

To Be Followed At 8.30, By A NEW VERSION of That
POPULAR COMIC OPERA

LA FILLE DE

MADAME ANGOT.

Written by HENRY J. BYRON, Esq.

New Scenery by ... ... T. GRIEVE & SON

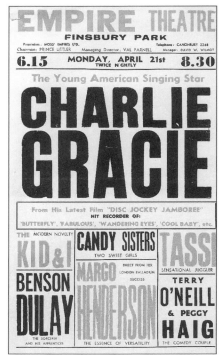

EMPIRE THEATRE

FINSBURY PARK

Proprietors : MOSS' EMPIRES LTD.   Telephone : CANONBURY 2248
Chairman : PRINCE LITTLER   Managing Director : VAL PARNELL   Manager : DAVID W. WILMOT

6.15   MONDAY, APRIL 21st   8.30
TWICE NIGHTLY

The Young American Singing Star

CHARLIE

GRACIE

From His Latest Film "DISC JOCKEY JAMBOREE"
HIT RECORDER OF:
'BUTTERFLY', 'FABULOUS', 'WANDERING EYES', 'COOL BABY', etc.

THE MODERN NOVELTY | CANDY SISTERS | TASSI
KID & I | TWO SWEET GIRLS | SENSATIONAL JUGGLER
BENSON | MARGO | DIRECT FROM HER LONDON PALLADIUM SUCCESS | TERRY O'NEILL
DULAY | HENDERSON | & PEGGY HAIG
THE SORCERER AND HIS APPRENTICES | THE ESSENCE OF VERSATILITY | THE COMEDY COUPLE

On the left, an early Royal Philharmonic Theatre Programme. The theatre in Islington High
Street later became the 'Grand' and was burnt out no fewer than four times. Right: A latterday
bill from the Finsbury Park Empire shows the incursions made by 'pop' culture into Variety in
the late 1950s.

The Cinematograph Theatre, Finsbury Park – entrance in Seven Sisters Road next to the park
gates. An adjoining skating rink was part of the complex. The cinema was still known popularly
as the 'Rink' long after the skating had gone.

Highbury Picture Theatre
near Highbury Corner.

The film studios in
Highbury New Park about
1929.

Islington Film Studios were located by the Regents Canal. Taking over an old warehouse building they became a very important centre of film making in this country.

Finsbury Park in 1832.

Finsbury Park in 1832 when the area was known as Hornsey Wood. The New River is seen flowing through the fields and trees. It was a leisure retreat in the countryside with the Hornsey Wood tavern providing refreshments.

Finsbury Park Gates

The main gate of Finsbury Park. The open space was laid out as a formal park after house-building had begun to fill the fields with streets.

Finsbury Park Conservatory – a typical feature of parks of the Victorian and Edwardian eras.

In 1912 the park boasted not only a lake and neatly laid out paths but also a convenient bookstall.

Six
Crime and Punishment

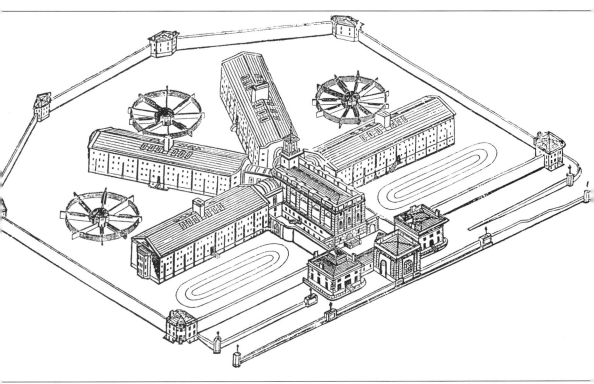

A bird's eye view of Pentonville Prison, built in 1840.

A corridor at Pentonville. Originally known as a model prison, the separate system of confinement led to mental illness among the inmates who received little human contact.

A most horrid and bloody

MURTHER

COMMITED

AT

ISLINGTON

In the

COUNTY

OF

MIDDLESEX

On Saturday the 7th of Inftant *July* 1683. by Four Foot-padders whereof two are taken whofe names are *Thomas Wilfon* and *Neal Johnfon*, the laft being the man that committed the murther upon the body of the deceaf- ed; who dyed of his wounds, in the fpace of five hours notwithftanding all meanes ufed to the contrary

'Murther Committed' – an early pamphlet about the discovery and apprehension of murderers in the town.

THIS IS "THE HOUSE" THAT MAN BUILT,

AND this is the home
of the poor Suffragette,
And there's room for
a great many more
in it yet;
When they racket
and riot
And will not keep quiet,
We place them on plank
beds and very low diet;
To stop all their din
We just run them in,
Into THIS HOUSE
that man built.

Holloway Prison in 1905. Originally opened as a male/female penitentiary, it was later converted into a gaol for females in 1903. It figured prominently in the newspapers during the Suffragette struggles.

An anti-Suffragette postcard, 'This is the house that man built'.

Hawley Harvey Crippen has become one of the most celebrated murderers in English criminal history. Living in a house which was coincidentally a very short distance from Islington's two prisons, he was eventually convicted of the murder of his wife, whose remains were finally discovered buried in the cellar of their home at 39 Hilldrop Crescent.

The overbearing Belle Elmore (her stage name as a rather unsuccessful music-hall actress) otherwise known as Cora Crippen. She was never seen again after a dinner party at her home on 31 January 1910. Dr Crippen said she had gone off to America. Her friends did not believe this and voiced their suspicions to Scotland Yard, who at first could come up with no answer to the mystery.

Crippen and his mistress, Ethel Le Neve, stand in the dock at Bow Street Police Court on their return to England. Alarmed by a police search of 39 Hlldrop Crescent, which had in fact revealed nothing, Crippen foolishly drew attention to himself by fleeing to Antwerp with Le Neve, whom he persuaded to dress as a boy, and from there taking ship to Canada. The captain of the *S.S. Montrose* was suspicious of the couple's affectionate behaviour and Le Neve's inadequate disguise and radioed to London. Inspector Dew boarded a faster boat and confronted the couple on 31 July 1910.

CRIPPEN'S HOUSE, 39 Hilldrop Crescent, London, N.
With Sandy McNab, the new owner, standing at gate,

Sandy McNab, a theatrical self publicist, bought the house with its grim memories and made the most of the great public interest after Crippen was found guilty and hanged. Ethel Le Neve was tried separately as an accessory but found not guilty and released.

Seven

Temples of Commerce

Flower sellers line up for the camera in their traditional dress at Chapel Market by the Angel, Islington.

Williams and Company, fishmongers, 110 Seven Sisters Road, in 1912. George Chapman, later the manager, stands on the left.

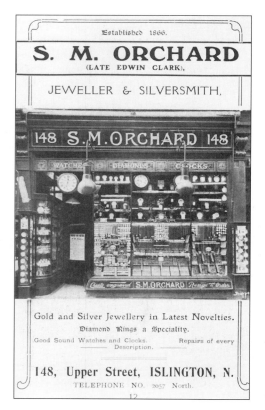

S.M. Orchard took over the jewellers business at no. 148 Upper Street from Edwin Clark, whose family founded it in 1866.

On the left, the Holloway Art Gallery run by J.W. Hancox, carver and gilder, at 92–94 Seven Sisters Road; and, right, how cosy Dell's Cafe, Holloway Road, looks with its then up-to-date Art Nouveaux appearance and style in mantlepiece, tables, screen, and electolier lighting.

The busy Holloway Road shopping centre at the Nags Head in 1904. Horse trams and buses compete for passengers.

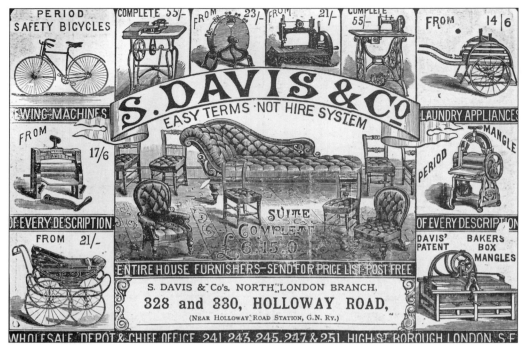

S. Davis advertise common household equipment of the day at the turn of the century.

A typical Welsh dairy at 297–9 Upper Street. There was at one time an abundance of such dairies run by Welsh folk which supplied milk to Islington and North London. The upstairs premises is the Holly Bush Hotel, which provided another outlet for the shop provisions.

Evans North London Domestic Stores, Caledonian Road billhead, 1920. Thomas Samuel Evans worked for Heals for a short time as a lad, but had then vowed never to work for anyone else and set up this shop making items of domestic furniture, with some bought in. Small kitchen tables with a drawer to keep the cutlery in – most families ate in shifts in working class districts – were the main stock in trade. These were delivered to customers on a wheelbarrow by one of Evans' sons until they left school.

Herbert George Sidney Evans, the youngest son, in his Royal Engineers uniform, went off to the Great War to run the light railways in the French and Belgian battlefields. They took shells and ammunition up to the front line and brought back the corpses of dead soldiers for burial wherever possible. All of the five Evans boys went to work on the railway in peacetime while the shop was left to the parents and the hired help to run.

The Caledonian Cattle Market – a nineteenth-century print. The live cattle market was moved from Smithfield to Copenhagen Fields in 1855 – the Caledonian Road was on the drovers route to Smithfield.

A corner of the Cattle Market in the 1920s. This was held on Mondays and Thursdays.

Selling hens at the Caledonian Market, 1935.

Looking down the Caledonian 'antique' or general market from the gates, 1935. With the decline of the livestock market the general market was held on Tuesdays as well as Fridays.

Glass and gilt at the 'Cally' Market, 1935. Stolen goods and every other kind of saleable goods soon appeared on the 'Cally'. The Caledonian 'Silver Kings' became well known.

'On the stones' – almost every possible type of object found its way eventually to the 'Cally'.

Eight
The Northern Foothills

Electric trams, motor buses, and a cyclist whiz along under the rebuilt Highgate Archway about 1908, the year the first suicide took place from the parapet. The new bridge was opened in 1900.

The old Archway Tavern in 1872, between the two hills – the Highgate Hill route to the North and Archway Road, which was originally cut as a tunnel to make a better gradient for the Turnpike traffic.

Dick Whittington and his cat. The legend that Dick Whittington failed to make the grade in London and decided to leave but was turned back on hearing Bow Bells at Highgate Hill to ultimately find fame and success and become Lord Mayor, has only been traced back to 1605. It may date from 200 years after Whittington's death.

The Whittington stone, 1905, between Salisbury and Macdonald Roads. A sculpture of Dick's cat was commissioned in 1964 to sit on top of the stone. Due to vandalism and road improvements the stone has been moved near the corner of Magdalen Avenue.

St. Joseph's Retreat adds a colourful touch to Highgate Hill. Founded in 1858, work on this new building with its 107-foot-high dome began in 1888.

Maiden Lane Toll House in 1830, showing the boundary stones placed by the Parishes of St. Mary, Islington, and St. Pancras, on this corner of Islington on the road to Highgate Village.

Taking in the scene from the top of the Archway bridge, 1905. Moving along Hornsey Lane from Highgate Hill eastwards we pass over the bridge with Archway Road and its Edwardian traffic below.

The old stone Archway in summer around 1864, engulfed by foliage as viewed from the north side.

THE FOOTWAY
THROUGH
OLD HIGHGATE ARCH.

W. WEST.

The footway through the old Highgate Arch – a charming sketch of this area of which no photograph is available.

93

The old stone Highgate Archway from the south, with not a vehicle in sight, 1873.

The old arch being demolished, 1898/9, with the new arch above it.

A foggy day at the Archway in 1912. The scene is still dominated by horse traffic.

The impressive Holborn Infirmary at the foot of the hill in 1914.

At the bottom of Archway Road a familiar ritual of tram travel is enacted involving the change pit at the the terminus. Plenty of staff are in attendance and a nice traffic jam is building up behind the tramcar.

Nine

Highbury Heroes

A delightful Arsenal team line-up in 1927 taken when they had reached the Cup Final for the first time. Although they lost to Cardiff City this event marked their coming of age in the big time and justified the move to Highbury fourteen years before. The 1930s were to be marked by success after success and the club once had seven players in the England Team. Left to right: Blyth, John, Cope, Kennedy, Parker, Lewis, Seddon, Butler, Baker, Hulme, Brain, Hoar, Buchan (Capt.). An odd record was held by Alf Baker – he was the only Arsenal player in history to have filled all eleven positions at different times.

Telegraphic Address — "GUNNERITIC, FINSPARK, LONDON."   **Registered Office —AVENELL ROAD GILLESPIE ROAD, N.**

Woolwich Arsenal Football & Athletic Co.,
LIMITED.

Secretary and Manager: Colours:
GEORGE MORRELL.   **RED SHIRTS, WHITE KNICKS.**

Directors:
H. G. NORRIS, J.P. (Chairman), W. HALL, C. D. CRISP, G. E. DAVIS, J. W. HUMBLE.

THE BANNER IS STILL FLYING and we sincerely hope to enrol you as one of our ever-increasing procession of loyal supporters. Let our new ground at Highbury be your favourite football rendezvous. Rest assured you will get good football in return for your generous patronage.

'The banner is still flying'. Woolwich Arsenal moved to Highbury in a remarkable act of faith, deserting their previous home at Plumstead, S.E. London. The first programme at the new ground is full of optimistic appeals. The club were desperate to secure better crowds and results. This first game against Leicester Fosse was won 2-1.

A WORD FROM MANAGER MORRELL.

The Editor of the Programme, which I hope the supporters of the Woolwich Arsenal Club will always regard as the connecting link between themselves and the management, has asked me to write a few notes by way of greeting to those who, by their presence here to-day, show that they are interested in the welfare of the old club.

To those of you who have only the slightest knowledge of the troubles and pitfalls which bestrew the path of the present day professional football club, it must be obvious that Woolwich Arsenal has had more than its share of bad luck in seasons past. As the first professional league club in the South, we have had a record of which we can feel proud, and the fact that we failed to hold our place in the First Division last season is more reason for sympathetic commiseration than for even the mildest condemnation of anybody concerned.

The modern means of transport and the great growth of other clubs put Plumstead out of the reckoning as a football centre for the vast body of London enthusiasts. Now we are here, in a new home which, in the course of a few weeks, will be second to none in its general appointments. I look to the future with the greatest optimism. We are all out to go back to the First Division. Whatever men Woolwich Arsenal need, will be got if it is at all possible. In the team at our disposal I have every confidence. They are a lot of good fellows, who are determined to do all they can to win success. I do not think we need have much fear in comparing our defence with that of any of our opponents, and we are hoping that Jobey and Hardinge will maintain their form. If they do, there will be no cause for complaint. Hardinge has been keeping himself fit by helping Kent to win the cricket championship, and who knows but what he may help to win another championship this season. I sincerely hope he will. Possibly, early failures need not discourage. With the loyal support of our followers, we will win through in the end, and ere long you will, I trust, see football at Highbury well worthy of the greatest city in the world.

GEORGE MORRELL.

'A word from Manager Morrell'. The new ground had originally been the sports ground of St. John's Hall, a training college for clergymen, and this was leased to the club.

The Arsenal team, 1920. Arsenal finished tenth in Division One in 1919/20 and ninth in 1920/21. Many spectators were travelling to the games via the underground railway – Gillespie Road station, later renamed Arsenal, was very close.

Arsenal, 1922. The team had slipped to seventeenth in season 1921/22 but came back to eleventh position in 1922/23.

(Left) H.A. White made 102 appearances between 1920–30 scoring forty goals in Division One as well as five in Cup games – the kind of club player who kept Arsenal on course for greater things in the League and F.A. Cup. (Right) Billy Blyth's career spanned the years 1915–29. He played in 314 League games, scoring 45 goals, and 29 F.A. Cup matches, scoring six goals. He was another of the players who established the club in the First Division after their re-election in 1919.

Arsenal win the cup, 1930. Tom Parker, the skipper, holds the cup while Joe Hulme is to his right and Eddie Hapgood on his far right.

Rebuilding the team, Arsenal began to accumulate some outstanding talents. James and Bastin, England players, 1932.

Three more of Arsenal's England internationals, Hulme, Jack, and Lambert, also in 1932.

Arsenal win the League Championship – their golden era is now well under way. Also in the picture is the F.A. Charity Shield, which they won five times in the 1930s: 1930/1, 1931/2, 1933/4, 1934/5 and 1938/9.

The Arsenal team of 1935/6 season. They had just won the First Division for the third successive time.

Winners of the 1936 Cup Final. The Captain, Alec James, is chaired by his colleagues. George Allison, the Manager, is second from left at the front.

Building on success, August 1908. A pre-season practice match is being played as the new stand nears completion in the background.

Ten
Railways Change the Pattern

Platform One, Kings Cross main line terminus of the Great Northern Railway about 1912. One of the early lines into London, many of its routes were express services to the north of England. A separate section of the station became the terminus for suburban services. North of the station the lines made their way through Islington, with one main station in the borough, after the early days, at Finsbury park.

A dramatic shot of a group of locomotives around the turntable in the loco shed at Kings Cross, about 1907. The turntable enabled trains to be marshalled effectively in and out of the terminus.

Crouch End Railway Station in the days of strict order, about 1907. It served commuters from Islington's northernmost suburbs.

The North London Railway station at Mildmay Park, about 1906. The first station inside the borough on this route from the east, which looped through the borough, connecting it with Hampstead, Kew, and West London, as well as the City of London.

Cabbies ply their trade outside Canonbury station, the next stop westwards on the N.L.R. In Edwardian times, many prosperous financiers and businessmen lived nearby.

The grand façade of Highbury Station on the North London Railway around 1908, hints at its relative importance. The frontage incorporated numerous commercial premises, and the Cock Tavern is on the left. The business traffic between Upper Street and Holloway Road swirled ceaselessly around the Highbury Corner junction behind and to either side of the camera.

Barnsbury, the final station in the L.N.R.'s westward progress through the borough, about 1906. The site of the station has been altered several times and access is now again in the Caledonian Road, instead of in Roman Way, as shown here.

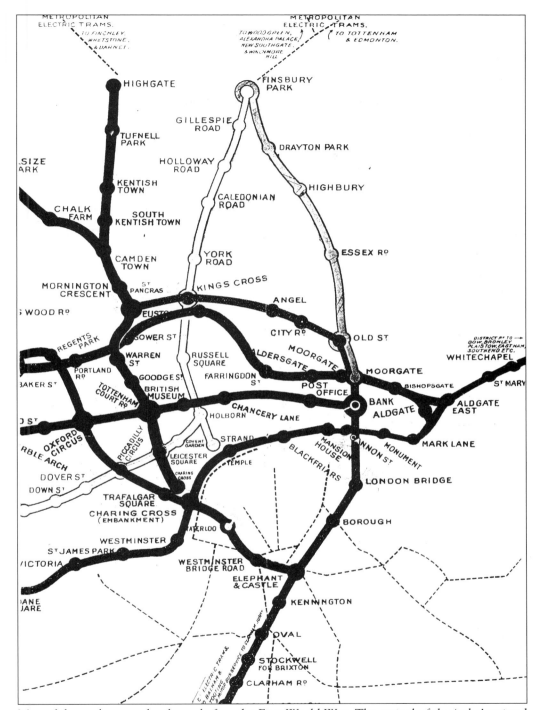

Map of the underground railways before the First World War. The arrival of the 'tube' assisted the commercial boom in Edwardian Islington. Four tube lines had stations within its boundaries.

A London Tube Station, (Great Northern & City Rly.)

Great Northern and City railway scene. This line ran under the borough from Finsbury Park via Drayton Park, Highbury, and Essex Road to Old Street and Moorgate. It had originally been meant to carry the Main Line trains from above ground down into the City and the tunnels were built much bigger than other 'tubes'.

GREAT NORTHERN. PICCADILLY & BROMPTON Ry. SHIELD in/in CONSTRUCTION.

The grandly named Great Northern Piccadilly and Brompton Railway under construction using the shield method. There were stations at Finsbury Park, Gillespie Road (later renamed Arsenal), Holloway Road, Caledonian Road, and York Road.

Nell Smith, ticket collector and later lady booking clerk on the Great Northern and City Railway at Highbury and Finsbury park Stations, poses in her new uniform in the 1920s.

Typical electric motor passenger car on the G.N.P. & B. Railway.

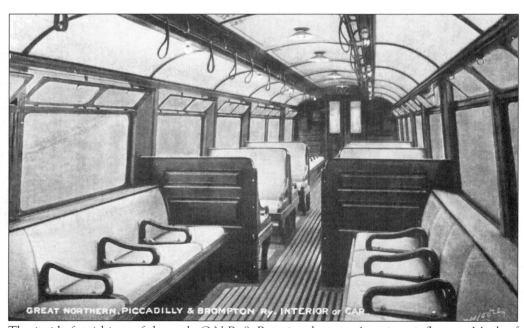

The inside furnishings of the early G.N.P. & B. trains show an American influence. Much of the money for early tube lines in London was raised in the U.S.A.

Eleven

Wheels Along
the Road

London General, Garden Seat, Horse Bus outside the Angel station of the City & South London railway. Horse Bus services were thriving in late Victorian London. The population was at its height and a large proportion used the various forms of public transport.

The London Road Car Company's Hornsey Rise and Sloane Square bus in the 1880s. A Union Jack flies at the front.

'Favorite' horse bus outside the Agricultural Hall, at which the Royal Military Tournament is advertised, about 1905.

The Favorite route ran between the Archway Tavern and London Bridge station via Holloway and Highbury.

A smartly attired conductor on the tiny platform of the Holloway and Fulham bus with his hand ready on the bell wire.

A lay 'clippie' during the First World War, on the back of a motor bus on the No. 19 route. The shape of the vehicle has subtly changed with the conversion from real horsepower to motor.

Developments in motorbus design led to this NS type, seen here on the No. 14 route which travelled through Islington from Hornsey Rise via the Caledonian Road to Kings Cross. This route remained the same until very recent years.

An early horse tram passing Loraine Place in Upper Holloway.

The new electric cars of the Metropolitan Electric Tramways at Finsbury Park Gates. On 22 July 1904, the first routes from Finsbury Park to Wood Green and Manor House to Seven Sisters Corner, were opened.

Highbury Station single deck tram.

An atmospheric view of trams at Finsbury Park in 1922. A bus on Route 78 pulls out from Blackstock Road in front of a tram.

A prototype tram – Bluebird of 1932, numbered No. 1, in the Central Repair Depot about 1934.

Trams on Route 35 awaiting their return journey to Forest Hill via the Kingsway Subway at the Archway Terminus, about 1946.

Tram 2000 negotiates the tight curve from Dove Road to Southgate Road in the late 1940s – one can almost hear the screeching of the wheels on the rails. The old nameplate with Dorset Street crossed through can just be seen. The street was renamed in 1935 in honour of the famous Islington building firm Dove Bros, 110 years after it had been constructed.

Heavy traffic at Holloway Road, Nags Head, in 1938. This picture clearly shows how tram passengers took their lives in their hands crossing between pavement and vehicle when alighting and boarding.

A tram accident holds up traffic in the Seven Sisters Road, in the mid-1930s

Acknowledgements

The author would like to thank the following:
L. Moholy-Nagy, London Transport, Owen Routledge.